I'M

GONNA

TELL

I'M GONNA TELL

...AN OFFBEAT TALE OF SURVIVAL

Lori Cardille

Writer's Showcase

San Jose   New York   Lincoln   Shanghai

I'm Gonna Tell
...an offbeat tale of survival
All Rights Reserved © 2001 by Lori Cardille

Writer's Showcase
an imprint of iUniverse.com, Inc.

For information address:
iUniverse.com, Inc.
5220 S 16th, Ste. 200
Lincoln, NE 68512
www.iuniverse.com

ISBN: 0-595-14203-6

Printed in the United States of America

This book is
dedicated to you,
my fellow survivors;
to help you begin
to laugh
again.

From my disfigured,
yet full heart.
I love you.
Lori

ALL OF THE ILLUSTRATIONS in this book were drawn by the author, Lori Cardille. She calls her cartoons Humoroons, or Philosophical Thoughts in a Box. Lori also thinks that they would make terrific postcards.

THE PHOTOGRAPHS were taken by the author as well, with the exception of the picture of Lori on page 69, which was taken by Diane from a photography class and Lori would thank her if she knew her last name. The First Communion pictures were beyond Lori's control.

The blank pages throughout this book are intended for your own writings and drawings.

Acknowledgments
I WANT TO THANK…

My parents for believing me when I finally told. My husband, Jim Rogal, who rode the roller coaster from hell with me. My children, Kate and Jake, my brother, Bill, my sister, Marea, my in-laws, Ann and Alvin Rogal, and the other Rogals, my cousin, Cynthia Barr, for sharing herself and her memories so lovingly, Margaret Nunberg, who taught me how to love, Dr. Ruth Eissler, Dr. Ted Becker, Dr. John Hitchcock, Dr. Bolonovitch, Dr. Mitzle, Nancy Hile, Grace Martin, Dr. Al Corcoran and Pittsburgh Action Against Rape. My best friends, Mary Beth Davis-Rogers, Jill Fine, Mary Ann Hepp-Basilone, Karen Meyers, Nina Gram-Humphrey, Amy Uriah, Sue Falvey, Michael Jacobs, Barry & Lois Zwibel, Sharona Fae, Susan Prothroe, Chris Potocki, Marina Posvar Green, Roberta Farkas, Robert Telleria, Rabecca Einhorn, Dr. Robert Einhorn, Sally Miles, Dave Nixon, all of my friends of Bill's. To the investigators who understood my fear of being killed. Thanks to my Hospice family, all of you, especially Mary Friday, Jean Robinson, Carrol Mackey…my mentors, my protectors.

A very special thanks to Gail Hunter for encouraging me to write it all down and to Dr. Jerry Rabinowitz for sticking with me.

A prayer of thanks to all the angels who stroked my hair and gave words of encouragement, who shared their stories, who cried with me, you know who you are.

And—believe or not—thank you, Uncle Bob, for without your abuse I wouldn't have become the "me" I am today.

Preface
THE REASON

The fact that my life would make me a good guest on a talk show makes me feel shame. Yet I have come to the point that I have suffered greatly. I have laughed like a hyena through my life's sorrows. I have cried so hard and long, I never thought I would stop. I have been a sinner and a saint.

I have written this book for the love of myself and you. Because of my uncle, whom I trusted and loved, feared and despised, I was a victim of extreme sexual and mental abuse.

I am finally not embarrassed to call myself that weak word: victim. I am a victim and I have a story to tell. I hope to give laughter to those who suffer and can relate. I am a proud survivor.

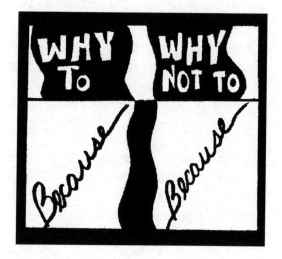

Perfection

When the priest used to come into my second grade class, in 1962, it was quite an event. The nun would blush and become even more perfect. The class would know we were to be on our best behavior and we all tried to show off how "good" we were. We were so good you could choke on the goodness in the air. We were being shown off like trained seals, "good" trained seals, seals with halos.

A few questions of catechism would be asked and we would respond...goodly. Inevitably the nun would ask us seals, "Now, who would like to become a priest or a nun when you grow up?" Of course all of us raised our flippers with such zeal, like "good" seals. I suppose I raised mine, just to fit in, but ohhhhhh I wanted, wanted so desperately wanted not to be a nun. I wanted to bypass that silly stage, I WANTED TO BE A SAINT! – a levitating, miracle-doing, vision-seeing, chaste, beautiful, special-powered, yet humble, saint. I took my catholic teachings quite seriously and prayed and prayed and played praying.

One day I was feeling particularly saintly, so I gently kissed and buried some rosary beads in the dirt next to my home. I got down on my knees and prayed that if I ran around the house three times, the beads would somehow vanish. This would be a sign for me that I was already a saintlet. I'll bet you're wondering if the beads were still there...?

I'll tell you later.

Trapped

The "Song Of Bernadette" was a great movie to eight-year-old me. It was about the Blessed Mother appearing to three small children on a regular basis. The children were transported to a blissful state when they saw her. They would receive messages from her, and these were secrets that only the Pope could know.

I remember making a grotto in the woods. It was a place to pray and play holy games. I fashioned rosary beads artistically out of poison red berries. I made a kneeler out of a few 2-by-4's and made a beautiful alter of devotion to Mary, with lilacs, lilacs, lilacs, surrounding the alter. I would kneel there and wait for visions. I'd squint my eyes and think, maybe that was a vision...ohh...ohh...I think I saw something float past my left eye.

I never prayed for things or even for life to change. There were horrific things happening to me, but that was all part of it. The life of a saint was hard. The more difficult and confusing it was, the more likely I would be to reach my goal.

At St. John's Elementary School, we started off the day by going to mass with our classes. This was right up my alley, I adored it...until one third grade mass morning when everything changed.

I thought it all happened because of the blue dress I had on. I never wore that dress again. I had just received communion, remembering not to bite the wafer so that it would not bleed in my mouth. I was offering up my prayers for something saintly, when all of a sudden my 50-pound body felt like it weighed at least 1,000 pounds. Everything around me felt like cotton. The painted mural, to the left of the alter – St. John The Baptist's head on a plate, being presented to King Herod – was for the first time in all my eight years a painting that scared the hell out of me. The beautiful statue of Christ on the cross, in the center of the alter, his muscular body

3

with a diaper on and his ceramic guts spilling from his side, became grotesque to me…and I couldn't breathe. I was sitting in the middle of the pew and I was trapped, with no breath because of the cotton air. Trapped by the guts and the decapitated head that was on a plate for dinner. Trapped by Mary Lou on my left and Bobby Joe on my right. I had to escape. I had to somehow run out with this body that I thought was still mine. Somehow I managed to float, in slow-motion, down the aisle, until I got to the back of the church and I thought, "Oh, this is what girls feel like when they faint." I hurled my body to the floor, still conscious. The teacher, Ms. McCulo, hated me (that's OK, because I was told culo in Italian means ass, and even if she hated me, I was a saintlet and I forgave her). She rushed back to see where St. Lori was running to. She made me put my head between my legs, which confused me even more. All that I can tell you is that MY LIFE WAS NEVER THE SAME AFTER THAT EXPERIENCE! If this was the mystical happening I was seeking, then I would become a devil worshiper on the spot. What the hell was going on?

Today I know that it wasn't the blue dress. Today I know about conversion hysteria, anxiety attacks, depression, break-downs, addiction, nine years of psychoanalysis, hospitalizations, transcendental meditation, E.S.T, just regular therapy, anti-depressants, screwed up relationships…and I sure know a little more about prayer.

I know now that it was Uncle Bob threatening my life with pictures of dead children and fetuses in formaldehyde. He just didn't realize that saints can take a lot and, like the children of Fatima, will never tell a secret…well…maybe to the Pope.

> Let nothing disturb Thee,
> Nothing affright Thee;
> All things are passing;
> God never changeth;
> Patience endurance.
> Attaineth to all things;
> Who God possesseth
> In nothing is wanting.
> Alone God sufficeth.
>
> ———
>
> St. Theresa of Avila,
> found on a bookmark in her Brevery

(The Mystic Vision) Harper, San Francisco

The overwhelming physical sensations I was experiencing distracted me from my saintly aspirations. I tried so hard to make sense of this event. If it wasn't the blue dress, maybe it was because I really needed to sit at the end of the pew, so I could escape! I needed to be able to escape, in case I would become...overcome...again. It sure was hard trying to get that aisle seat, when good child by good child was filing into the pews. I couldn't just hop in front of Jimmy or twirl back three people, to that precious, safe...oh so safe aisle seat. I had to follow the perfect line, as my breath became shallow and my palms flowed like Niagara Falls. Ahhhhhhhhh...free...free... free to run just in case "that thing" happened to me again. Most of the time I would not get my Valium seat, and I suffered. I simply, truly, deeply, suffered. I was so afraid of the fear that, almost on a daily basis, I would end up running to the back of the church, time and time again, Miss Ass in tow.

The saddest part of all of this was that I stopped listening to what was truly beautiful. The gorgeous Latin chants, the mystical smelling incense, my communion with God. Now I was just trying to survive and I felt so odd and different, the start of a life long belief that I was crazy.

It started to permeate my life. I stopped eating breakfast. I received a note from my doctor, Uncle Bob, to excuse me from joining in with my class.

Diagnosis: I had a "condition." So I would go to my classroom and sit alone and wait for the "sane" classmates, who wanted to be nuns and priests, to come back from mass. I was now a freak to myself. I would just sit there – I would just...sit there...alone. I would look around the room and wait. I knew this was odd, that I was odd, an odd ball. Maybe I could be patron saint to "the odd." Maybe that's what all this meant.

I used to love to play outside with my cousins. We lived in the city and they lived on my block. We would play, play, play, chase, kickball, basketball. Play tornado nine, a game in which we girls were rescued by Roy Rogers from a tornado outside the garage. I remember always loving to laugh when I played. I love and still love and will always love to laugh...at everything! Nothing is sacred to me. So one play day, while I was laughing, and flailing my eight-year-old body about, IT happened! While I was PLAYING! Oh God, Oh God. I fell to the ground and my cousins kept asking, "What's wrong Lori?" to which I replied, "I can't walk." They lifted my skinny body onto a red wagon, and the Red Flyer became an ambulance.

I must digress a bit to tell you just how skinny I was. Cruelly, a classmate in the schoolyard called me a faggot. I didn't know what this word meant, so I looked it up in the dictionary and it said, "a clump of sticks or twigs." Made sense, I was a faggot child, skinny as a stick. An odd faggot child.

My cousins zoomed my little faggot body to my mother who took me to the doctor, who happened to be my uncle. My mother carried me into his house because I was so frozen that I would not walk, so hysterical I couldn't see, and so confused. Somehow I knew through this chaos that I didn't want to see that uncle for some reason, even though he was my doctor and revered by all of those around him because he was a DOCTOR! And we were all uneducated, Polish immigrants who came to Erie, PA from the old country. We were poor and inferior, yet we had lots of love and lots of faith. But Dr. Bob was a doctor. How lucky we were to have him to take care of us poor Polish peasants from Beowistock. Be grateful!

Uncle Bob knew the scoop, he knew his power, he had his gig down. He was thought to be a kind doctor because he volunteered his time to the Gertrude Barber Home for Retarded Children and to the Erie school system.

So my mom carried my little twig body into his house and gently handed me to him. Here is what he proceeded to do: he put my stick body on the floor, on my back, then he sat on me. He literally sat on top of my stomach and he smacked me over and over on my face (this is how we poor Polish people thought good doctors treated this condition). I was trapped, yet at that same moment, I became quiet. I do not mean just silent; I mean I went to the deepest, softest, gentlest, most meditative quiet part of my soul. I found my safety, and as I look back, that is when God held my hand.

The abuse continued for a couple more years. Bob reassured my parents that little girls always break their hymens on bicycles. Whenever I showed any symptoms, he doctored me…and so it goes with many victims of this terrible crime…God bless us all.

If I ascend up into heaven, Thou art here:
If I make a bed in Hell,
Behold, Thou art there.
If I take the wings of the morning
And dwell in the uttermost
Parts of the sea,
Even there shall Thy hand lead me,
And Thy right hand shall hold me.

(Psalm 139)

Chilly Billy's Daughter

Some children's fathers work for the post office, some are doctors, others business-men. My father worked as Chilly Billy. Anyone growing up in the 1960's and 70's in Pittsburgh knows exactly who Chilly Billy is and what he means to them. My dad is a legend, an institution in Pittsburgh. Recently, comedian Dennis Miller, who grew up in Pittsburgh, spoke at the Museum of Television and Radio in New York. He was asked what three people influenced him the most in his career. My dada, Chilly, was one of those three people.

Chilly Billy was the host of a show called Chiller Theater, the first of its kind in this country. Every Saturday night at 11:30, children across the 'Burgh begged their par-ents to let them stay up to watch Chiller Theater. Dad was cool and funny, corny, off-beat and elegant.

He also hosted a real steel town show called Studio Wrestling. These were the days before Hulk Hogan and Jesse "the Body" Ventura. These were the days of Bruno Samartino, Killer Kowalski, Haystacks Calhoon and George "the Animal" Steel. These huge men were all friends of my father, so I would walk into the house and Bruno or Haystacks would be eating dinner with the family. Jumpin' Johnny Defazio would stop by for dessert. This was a real kick once we were all together as a family in Pittsburgh. But for several years — the nightmare years of Uncle Bob and uncontrollable anxiety — Chilly Billy lived in Pittsburgh and the rest of us lived in dreary Erie. My dad wasn't there, another reason I felt trapped and alone. We moved back together as a family in 1965. I was thrilled, not only to be a family again, but also to be far far away from Uncle Bob.

My new world was safe, but it was highly unusual being Chilly Billy's daughter!

Fame is fame and I don't care if it's international, national, or local…people react to the famous in an absurd way.

Whenever we were out, my dad was mobbed as we, his family, waited patiently while he signed autographs and schmoozed with his fans. He loved it and they loved it – me?? I was proud and confused – so what else is new? When we first moved back, I tried out for that then cool, now strange position of cheerleader. I heard a voice from the crowd say, "She just got it because SHE'S CHILLY BILLY'S DAUGHTER!" STINGGGGGG! This moment started a whole new neurosis in the anxiety ridden, saintly, abused, good, humble Lori.

From the
philosophical dictionary

Chilly Billy

The Good Years in Suburbia

High school I remember as one silly laughing fun time, with anxiety attacks added in for spice. I went to an all-girl Catholic High school, Vincentian High. Two of my friend became lifelong soul mates. We found that we experienced life the same way: that things were absurd and silly; yet we believed in a Higher Force. We were wild, don't get me wrong, it's not like we were the head of the "Christians for Jesus" after-school club. Mary Beth and Mary Ann and Lori Ann were class clowns, mischievous kids, wetting our underpants from laughing. We shared a certain freedom that comes from being in a single sex school. Some of the attitudes of the nuns were just hilarious! It was a great time for me. I played sports galore. They used to call me "stretch" as co-captain of the basketball team. My uncle was far away. Mom was the mom of all moms: the safe mom to me and all my teenage friends, the mom who drove everybody around, to the mall, the ice skating rink, back and forth to friends' houses. My dad was Chilly Billy, handsome Denny Devlin was my boyfriend.

Life was good.

What Should I Be When I Grow Up???

(FORGOT TO THINK ABOUT THAT ONE.)

I performed in my senior class play…made the audience laugh…felt good…I decided to try out for one of the best drama schools in the country, Carnegie Mellon University, better known as CMU. All the applicants to CMU must submit themselves to a grueling audition process. The Drama Department auditions thousands of kids from around the country and chooses 50 for the freshman class. Thank God I had no idea what I was submitting myself to, I just liked it when that 12th grade audience laughed at me. For the audition, I had to pick out a monologue to perform. I naively chose a Strindburgh piece, difficult for even an accomplished actress. They stopped me in the middle of my masterpiece – how dare they, I thought, while I also thought about throwing up. They asked me to describe my living room at home, which I did (REMEMBER…TRAINED SEAL). They then proceeded to ask me two questions: first, "What would you do if you don't become an actress?" To which I answered, off the top of my head, "become a stewardess!" I had never thought of doing that in my entire life; besides, I didn't want to divulge my saintly aspirations. They also asked me what other schools I applied to. I snapped back quickly, "NYU." They replied, "GOOD SCHOOL! You should think of going there." Somehow I was accepted to CMU, guess they needed a stewardess type. Of the 50 or so that got in, I was one of the 12 who graduated four years later. Go figure.

Giving Birth

It was positively fate that CMU launched me into myself and the theater. Especially myself. With practically no theatrical experience under my belt, I was thrust amongst a crowd of 18-year-old actors who spoke high British for effect and had sex with the professors because this was the 70's and that was acceptable. Despite having been exposed to sex at a very early age, I believed myself to still be a virgin, a good Catholic virgin. I would remain that until the day I married. In fact if I were really serious about sainthood, I would keep my virginity all through my marriage, like St. Cunnagunda did in "The World According to Sister Bernarda."

Following the repressed and suppressed theme of my personality, Carnegie Mellon Drama Department was like Sodom and Gomorrah. One had to be invited back every semester. Being as shy as I was and out of place, I thought I was a goner. So did the hierarchy, I thought. Oh, but what was I to do? Who was I to be? One day, I had my shining moment to show how capable I was of breaking through this shy thing and becoming "open and available" so I could be taught how to become a true actress.

It was in the freshman acting class of Israel Hicks, a big, beautiful, strong, intimidating as hell, African American man. I think we were writhing around on the floor, freshman acting style, moaning and groaning, so we could all be free and open. Israel must have noticed my little shy moans and jerks and stopped this scene of hell and shouted "CARDILLE, GET IN FRONT OF THE CLASS! I want you to spread your legs in front of this class and give birth." I meekly asked, "may I keep my clothes on?" he hesitated, then said, "yes." So, shyly, yet with determination, I broke loose and gave birth. I was the proud mother of a cute, new...me. Now that I was born, I could grow on to become a sophomore. I was like a turtle who came out of her shell to become Ethel Merman when necessary.

Not only did I learn to become a classical actress, I discovered that I could feel and express myself more on stage, in front of an audience, than I could in life. This is how my passion for my profession was born.

It was in an Israel Horowitz one act called Rat's that I knew for sure. I played Jebbie, the survivinest-of-the-fittest rat. I was teaching a young rat the ropes of how to survive in Scarsdale...not an easy place for a rat to survive. As the story progressed, it became a matter of my own survival, and I had to kill this young naive rat or be killed myself. I killed that little rat with such conflicted, complicated, powerful emotion that I went on to become a leading lady. From rat to Rosalind in Shakespeare's As You Like It. From Feydeau to Molière, all because I was trainable and because I could tap my rage, my sadness, my glee on that stage far away from my uncle. I was truly born into the theater at CMU. I was the survivinest of the fittest, like my dear rat friend Jebbie. For the next 15 years, I knew my place in the world. I was an actress, and a damn good one, and nothing was going to stop me!!!

So I moved to New York and did a Massingill Disposable Douche commercial.

The Edge...Of Night
The Edge...Of Insanity

Shortly after I pitched Massingill Disposable Douche, I landed my first major part on the very old and popular soap opera, The Edge Of Night. For two years I played Winter Austin, an ex-porno queen with a heart of gold, trying to make it platinum. Noble Winter. Sick Lori. Remember, I was a trained seal child, and a well trained actress who took my craft quite seriously.

There was a plot line coming up where one of my ex-porn managers was going to blackmail me with my past. We always knew a few weeks in advance what the plot was before it aired. He was going to rape me and I was going to kill him. Not a good scenario for a girl who was trying to repress her past (her real past). Follow me so far? Me, real Lori, was raped, and Winter Austin, fake Lori, was going to be raped, and to top it off, KILL, KILL, KILL my ex-porn manager. Well, let's just say the lines were crossing into my unconscious Erie mind. Anxiety, Valium, anxiety, Valium, anxiety, Valium Valium Valium. The anger I had to dredge up to "pretend" to kill this character was too much for this fractured soul of mine. I was emotionally hemorrhaging all over the place. I felt so crazy, soooooo crazy, you are soooooooo crazy he said, I know!!!! UNCLE,

I cry Uncle!

I called my lawyer and checked myself into Paine Whitney. I was convinced that I had ruined my career...until my agent told me not to worry, I was just added to his list of chic clients who broke down once in a while.

19

The producers of the show sent me flowers. It was better than Christmas, when we all got a bag of Procter and Gamble products from the sponsors. I might have been on the chic list, but I was one big confused failure in my mind.

As I mentioned, the shows were taped a few weeks in advance, and as you can imagine, a lot of television is watched, or should I say stared at, in Paine Whitney. So guess who we all stared at every afternoon at 3:30? My big fat mug. In those days, the psychotics were mixed in with the depressed patients and the addicts, it was one mass unenlightened mess. "That's me!" I exclaimed, as my face would appear on TV, "That's me!" Some blank stares, some "oh yeah, sures," some "how bout dats" (from me). I just thought, this is so damn odd. What the hell is going on? Remember, these were the days before Prozac and Zoloft, Paxil and Waxil. They observed me for one week, no meds, nothing, and one day a conference was called with doctors and staff sitting at those funny desks that we used in third grade with me in the middle. "Lori, we think you need to know about who you are. You are a very bright girl who could use analysis." Psychoanalysis. What the hell is that? I wondered. Psycho, psycho, psycho analysis. What??? Five times a week? Holy shit I really am sick.

Soon, and with help from my very best friend, 80-year-old Margaret Nunberg; who happened to have played with Freud's children as a child in Vienna, and who knew all the best analysts, I was educated about the world of psychoanalysis in the person of Dr. Ruth Eissler. This was a wonderful and very difficult undertaking, yet I was determined to find out what was wrong with me.

Oh, by the way, ABC and CBS continued to hire me. You know — actor, crazy, what's the diff?

Muscles in group
therapy.

B.Y.O.B.
R.S.V.P.
A.S.A.P.
Q.R.S.T.
A.S.P.C.A... I Feel
... A dog... I feel
Like A dog... today.

$100 for 50 minutes of Free Association.

Awards... Nominations For Awards...Nominations For Nominations

Don't you think awards are rather goofy? I do. We are proud when we receive them, embarrassed to hang them, and in moments of drunkenness or some weird ego burst we brag about them! The tall towering shining tacky awards from the past that I keep on my shelf are silly to me today, yet I wept with pride and joy when they were presented to me.

I can tell you that I was in worldly heaven when I was given the honor of being selected May Queen, at that famous age of eight. This boosted my Saint ego to the point where I spoke only in a whisper (that's how Saints spoke, at least in the movies). May was the month in which Mary, the Blessed Mother, was honored. There were pageants and beautiful rituals to the Blessed Mother and I, the May Queen of the class, was needed. I carried a fragrant lilac crown on a silken pillow hand made by my grandmother, up the aisle in front of a procession of classmates as they sang, "Oh, Mary we crown thee with blossoms...today." I walked slowly, with great reverence to crown the translucent statue. With such holy reverence I strode, almost in a trance.

This is one of the first honors I remember receiving, a great highlight in my young spiritual life.

The next award I received was the American Legion Award. I wrote an essay on why I was proud to be an American. I received a $25 bond which I just recently cashed. I took my family to dinner and what a patriotic dinner it was. Then came the National Honor Society, co-captain of the basketball team, and, in the eight grade, I came in second for most popular. Joanne Gallagher was first.

When I was a junior at CMU I was nominated for a prestigious scholarship. Each department in Fine Arts nominated the most promising talent. Each of us (architect, musician, artist, opera singer, composer, actor) had to give a little speech about what we planned to do when we graduated. How awful to put us together in a room, trying to outdo each other with our future professions. How could we possibly compete against each other? The whole situation bothered me so. It was like Miss America. People were saying absurd things: they would teach the handicapped, or join the Peace Corps. They were kissing ass, there was no truth in the air. When they came to me, I had such a bad attitude that I spoke what I thought was the truth. I answered, "Well, I'll probably become a waitress when I move to New York." Cocky, yet truthful, me...I didn't get the scholarship.

When I was on The Edge Of Night I was nominated by the producers to be nominated for an Emmy. That's right, nominated to be nominated. Sounds good, kinda, means nothing. It's just the word, "Emmy," that sounds impressive, so I'll say it again, I was nominated to be nominated for an Emmy.

EMMY...EMMY...EMMY

I haven't won any awards lately, except the ultimate reward of knowing what it is like to love and be loved.

The Award That Makes
Me Feel Pride...

NINTH ANNUAL CAMPAIGN
The St. Francis Health Foundation

honors

Lori Cardille

AWARD NOMINEE

THE
COURAGE
TO COME
BACK.

ST.
FRANCIS
HEALTH
SYSTEM

Anyone who is so highly thought of by another
as to be seen as a model of courage and hope for others,
has already won a far greater prize than
we can even hope to give.

Sister M. Rosita Wellinger
President & Chief Executive Officer
ST. FRANCIS HEALTH SYSTEM

Rocky Bleier
Program Chairman
THE COURAGE TO COME BACK

David T. Dombrowiak
Chief Executive Officer
ST. FRANCIS HEALTH FOUNDATION

Lovers and
Other Victims

Lovers

God bless the men I've slept with. I'm sorry. The 70's were promiscuous times, in New York especially. All of my dear gay friends started to die. We were so confused, shell shocked. What the hell was going on? Friend after young friend died, our WWII. AIDS was going on, we found out later, too late for many. Dreaded sex, I hear you, Sister Bernarda, I hear, but I don't agree, at least not now. However, pre-analysis, I had an unconscious burning bush that was keeping my bush from burning. Yet I took on relationships, even if the person was all wrong for me. If I had sex once, I must marry this man. And so my poor boyfriends were haunted by my ghosts of Erie past. I did love you Denny, Arthur, Michael and Robert (despite your first name and the fact that you are a doctor). Some I liked, others I despised. I'm sorry. I tried the best I knew how, but I was cruel.

A Letter of Love to My Husband of 18 Years

Thank you my love for helping me through, for sticking around, for trying to unweave my web. I love you sweet lover, kind man. We almost drowned in our ocean of despair. Our mutual love and respect for each other pulled us through. Thank you for supporting my brutal honesty. I love you. I love to make love with you. We are so blessed.

I've Decided to
Be Nobody

Somebody, nobody, somebody, nobody, no body, no, I have a body, so I must be some-body. I was born Chilly Billy's daughter. I graduated from Carnegie Mellon, BFA, actress. Within a year, I was on the Edge of Night. Checking in with myself at that time, I was somebody on my way to become really somebody. During the next decade I did another soap, Ryan's Hope. I played on Broadway with Glenda Jackson and Jessica Tandy. I starred in a TV pilot. I did a slew of national commercials. Made lots of money. I starred in a major motion picture, George Romero's DAY OF THE DEAD, for which I won two Best Actress awards in international film festivals. I knew Leonard (Lenny) Bernstein personally. Yes, my agent had high hopes for this hard-working-try-ing-to-be-somebody.

I think I was driven by an Edward Gorey cartoon entitled, The Abandoned Sock. It's the life story of a sock that was blown off a clothes line. It seemed to have a serendipitous existence. After many adventures, it landed on a rosebush. It rained and snowed and rained and snowed until there was nothing left of the sock to speak of. Please don't let me be that sock! Studystudystudy. Workworkwork. Smile for the camera. BFA...BFA...CMU...CMU...I'm okay...yes, I'm okay. Then I had a child named Kate and I became a breast (at least I wasn't a sock). Although, you know, being a breast was the best thing for me, really. I would wake up and get ready to be Somebody and Kate would say, "I'm hungry, breast." This confused me terribly. In fact, this kept me terribly confused for the next seven years. One son Jake later, one move to back to Pittsburgh later, one nine-year Freudian analysis later, one, "No, I don't think I want to do that TV show now, because my daughter starts first grade this month and I want to drive her to school" later…Ohmygod Ohmygod Ohmygod…I'm a suburbanhouse wifemother! I'm a nobody! Quick Get back on track! The Road To Mecca at the City Theater. A wonderful part to show my stuff in Pittsburgh. Be Somebody in Pittsburgh. Sure! I'd love to play the part. But…then…after years of hard work, self-exploration, confusion, love and responsibility to others, I called the director of the play and said "Thank you so much, but I no longer consider myself an actress." For a while there, I thought I was going to be a sock, but you see, I've decided to be a mosaic. Somewhere along the line I decided to be nobody and it feels great!

The Suburban Cult Figure

Yep, that's me. I was the heroine in George Romero's DAY OF THE DEAD. Fans of this movie are rabid with their adoration of the film and with the character that I played, Dr. Sarah, one of the world's last surviving females, battling the zombies. And yep, I live in Pittsburgh and get fan mail; as I pick up my kids from school, prepare dinner, and volunteer here and there. Mother cult figure in Pittsburgh, PA. Conventions with thousands of fans, a strange event. I watch myself shyly sign autographs. Why the hell do they want my signature? I haven't done a film in years, yet I am an eternal cult figure. I live on in film, never aging, killing zombies forever. How strange, how split, how odd. Patron Saint of the odd – keeps coming up, how odd. I am a tough daughter of a bitch. You should see me with my Uzi. I shot you a few times too, Uncle zombie Bob. Oh well…life has always been ironic and strange and oh so wonderful.

Prayer for the Odd
We odd are not odd in the eyes of God.
Keep embracing your oddness.
Religions are odd.
The fact that we humans blink is odd.
All is odd, praise the Lod. Amen.

———

St. Lori,
Patron Saint of the odd.

John (Terry Alexander), Sarah (Lori Cardille) and McDermott (Jarlath
Conroy) arm themselves to enter an area filled with the living dead
in DAY OF THE DEAD, a Laurel Production from United Film Distribu-
tion Company.

Daring to be different in suburbia.

My Guru:
Mowhawk The Turtle

My 11 year old son, Jake, begged for his very own pet that he could love and cherish and call his son. Four cats, two dogs, and two ferrets were not enough. He needed his reptilian boy pet. So came Mowhawk, Jake's new buddy. I need to tell you that Mowhawk is an aquatic turtle, who can smell other-worldly at times. This adds to the true unconditional love one must have to care for such a thing. It has been three years now since Mowhawk has lived with us. He used to live in Jake's room, now he lives next to the washing machine. I've had conversations with Jake about what a wonderful life Mowhawk would have in a pond in the country. He responds with sobs and pleas of love for his son. It's as if I'm asking Jake to go live in the pond. I have not mentioned that for these three years, Jake does nothing to care for the slimy beast. He LOVES him though. "I love my Mowhawk mom!!!" In the meantime, Mowhawk has become a spiritual exercise for me and because of that one of my present gurus. When the student is ready, the teacher will appear. I just never thought it would be a turtle. I give him everything and he gives nothing back. I feed him, bathe his slimy body once in a while, talk to him, change his whole tank weekly — and yet if I put my finger near his mouth, he would snap it off in an instant. For the time being, Mowhawk gives me more than organized religion ever could. I've learned patience, tolerance, unconditional love; and I swear somewhere deep inside his turtle soul, he appreciates the fact that I am his sole caretaker, or his soul caretaker or he's my soul caretaker. I'm so confused oh silent Mowhawk, show me the way.

43

The holy space
of
Mowhawk

"For everything that lives is holy."
William Blake

Deep Sea Diving

I guess there's no need, since it's the late 90's, to explain that I was suppressing an atomic bomb of rage in my ocean. And that these anxiety attacks were variations of this impending explosion, and I was feeling the toxic bubbles surfacing. What I am grateful for is that my memories were so deeply repressed that I managed a fairly successful career, and the beginnings of a family life. It wasn't until my mid thirties, having had many varied and highly functional experiences, that the bomb blew up. I was thrown to the depths of my rage with all the sharks and eels, and I must say it was one bloody ocean.

But I have found that it is a vast ocean, with the survival of the fittest in peak performance, and I am lucky to be the guppy that survived my atomic ocean. I see swimming through this as a rather mystical experience. From saint to actress to mother to guppy. I knew despair, true hatred, and what it feels like to have a murderous heart. Long gone were the days of aspiring Sainthood, long gone was my belief in anything. I wanted to be dead, and I didn't care if I went to hell. I just couldn't be good anymore. I truly thought I would never stop crying, ever, ever, never, forever never stop crying. I found the solace and warmth of pills that saved me for a while – that is until they almost killed me. I went after my uncle with the law so ferociously that he can never practice medicine again. My husband left. Desperation. Numbness. Then, good riddance was all that I could muster. It was as if I felt every hurt, every penetration, every abandonment, all at the same time. This was a three-year period of a complete and needed meltdown.

I had to learn how to walk all over again. I had to learn that I was good, but not that good. Slowly, slowly building my way back with people who were human angels guiding me to see that it isn't black and white or even gray. Slowly I got the color to come back. Sometimes it was pure purple, sometimes light green, other times blackness with a touch of pink off to the side. Now mostly, it's pastels.

HA HA HA HA HA HA
HO HO HO HO
HEE HEE HEE
TEEHEE TEEHEE
OH BOY OH BOY
Ahh JEESE
sigh...
sigh...
sigh...
BOO HOO BOO HOO

Underneath the laughter...

Memory And Knowing:
Purging Uncle Bob

"I saw you, you bitch," he said, as he pulled me from the tiny hall closet where I hid, because I DID see! I saw you too asshole. Don't pull my hair, why did you hit me in the head? "Mommy, why is Uncle Bob giving you that shot?" "Uncle Bob, what are you doing to my mother?" "Get out of here, Lori, YOU ARE SUCH A WORRY WORT, you hissed." Jesus on the cross with his diaper on. St. John's head on a plate being offered as a gift…I can't breathe this cotton air…I can't breathe, and blood everywhere, as you sodomize me for seeing. Sodom and Gomorrah is in that bathroom. How did you hide the evidence?

ANKLES. I saw her lifeless dead ankles as he turned his head slowly to catch me catching. What are you doing to my mother? Memory or fantasy? Must save my family from what I see. Little girls smell like fish, you said, and I was your girl because your baby Michelle died and I am so happy for her to have you far away. Death is so safe from you. You, my doctor who diseased me and doctored me. Good thinking Bob, the ass that I loved and feared. God I hope you are working the night shift, so I can't feel your body against mine at night. You stink, I hate your Uncle Bob smell and I loved spending time on your 10-acre country house farm and I loved Bobby and Brian and your wife so much. We laughed and I felt so good with them. We played for hours in the deep woods on Tarzan vines and ventured down into the gully. Steep hills to go down and up, my faggot body conquered that hill as I slid on my bum that you sodomized – John the Baptist's head, blood, blood in church, in the bathroom, blood on the sacred

49

host if you bit it...I can't breathe this cotton air — aisle seat, the safe place to be so I could run from what I did not quite know then. Knowing now, after nine years of Freudian analysis with famous Dr. Ruth Eissler on West End Ave: Mom was sick, Dad lived away and you had me as your sexual rag doll. Like 'em young...ehhh ??? — 6,7,8,9?? Babies you loved too. "Let's go see the birdies," you would say, as you take us to the woods. Telling my sister's husband on their wedding day how she wasn't a virgin because you had had her, as you held up your baby finger. You held my baby Kate and said "I'm going to stick a needle in your tummy and you'll fly around the room like a balloon as the air comes out of your pee pee hole"...ha ha ha how funny...many laughed, from fear, as I stood frozen unable to save my Kate. Finally her father Jim said "What! are you crazy?" as he grabbed her away from you.

"Lori, yogurt helps yeast infections, put it up your-you-know-where." I stored it in the refrigerator and you warned all about the vagina yogurt...ha ha ha...and "scratch my back Lori," as you moaned with satisfaction while you read and ate at the kitchen table, while your terrorized Polish family kept quiet but all laughed...ha ha ha...at your sick vagina jokes. You had me, yep I wouldn't tell with dead children's pictures and warning me not to tell and pictures of dead men slaughtered from WWII...Blood blood, St. John's head on a plate...I can't breathe this cotton air..."what is wrong with me?" That eternal question — your doctor's fetuses in a jar, a good thing to show me to keep me quiet. Guess what I found out? That one of them was your sister's miscarriage...you Pol Pot you, you Hitler, you will go down in my history — that plaid shirt. "Why are you coming into the bathroom?" as I peed on the toilet...plaid shirt plaid shirt, as you made me kneel...plaid shirt plaid shirt, as you pulled my pony tail back and my head jerked backwards...plaid shirt, as this big ugly thing went into my mouth...blank out...throw up at the sink. How did I go on as if nothing happened, how could I hide this hideous torture? By anxiety attacks over and over and over through college and into adult-hood. You are just crazy!, I know I am, it's me that is crazy...screen blank — except — plaid shirt, I remember only plaid shirt anxiety panic panic for years and years, until I remembered. I wanted to get you with lawyers, the Licensing Bureau. What's this about being a pusher of drugs to teenage kids for sex? Then you turned state's evidence, turning in other doctors, walking away free, you knowing son of a bitch bastard asshole. FUCK YOU FUCK YOU FUCK YOU. No more sperm dripping down my mouth, you are caught and you can never practice medicine again; because if you renew your license for 25 dollars it will be taken away, because all know what you did to me...ha ha ha...you vagina joker. I know evil and it is you...I know the devil and it is you. Try to forgive, good Catholic girl – NO!! FUCK YOU UNCLE BOB!!! It's not me, slowly, It's not my fault!! I am not crazy. Slowly, years to understand, to put together. Thank you Bob for giving me a rich background of pain to make me love with deep compassion and hold the hands of hospice patients and cry with them in our private holy space.

Thank you for teaching me to hate myself so much and to learn my strength and self respect and love me...Lori Ann Cardille...Thank you, for my life is full and rich as I strive for goodness, because of you!!! I don't want to be in hell with you...I loved you. Why, I'll never understand, maybe it was a reverse of hate. Forgiveness?, we'll see, I do some days, can't others. I hope to forgive. I'm free, I'm free, I'm freeeeeeeeee, as your 80-year-old body prepares to meet your God. He will forgive because you were so sick with those damn amphetamines, you were sick, poor old Uncle Bob. God is good. Amen.   Amen, Amen,   Amen.

Lori Me Cardille

Lost Love

My Uncle Bob's family, his wife Lee, his children, Brian, Bobby and Mark, they are my most painful loss. I cannot talk about them without crying. Bobby and Brian have decided to treat me as if I am dead. Bobby and I were so close that we spoke the language of twins. One word meant ten paragraphs, one gesture meant an encyclopedia. Only we understood our codes.

Brian, I loved loved loved. A gentle soft person, an artist, now an accomplished doctor. Mark, he was much older and remote, I didn't know him well. I would just watch him with his muscular body filled with the rage of a bull. But Bobby oh Bobby oh Bobby, I miss you so. I miss your humor, your smile, our paper route that had the lady with the dog that said mama. I miss the poker games we played on floating rafts in the pool, I miss playing acey-deucy, and getting a nine and a Jack and impulsively yelling "Pot!," as we gathered the pennies in the middle. I miss shouting Annapurna, when a big wave in Wildwood would whip us to shore, sand sagging our bathing suits like a baby's diaper. Laughing and laughing at everything and nothing, at life's ironies and our pain. Dear Bobby, you must remember the train ride from Fire Island to Aunt Betty's funeral when we were both professionals in New York and we shared a berth and as usual we talked and talked. You asked me if I thought your dad had raped me and if I thought he could be a pedophile and I said I don't know because at that point I did not know all…yet. Remember, after you asked these questions, I vomited for the next three days through dear Aunt Betty's funeral? Remember your father picking us up at the train station and immediately starting his sexual jokes about kissing cousins sharing a berth? I remember that same day your father walking in on me while I was in my slip, while I ironed the funeral dress and I ran to the toilet when he left the room and continued to vomit, to clear my body so that I could forget.

What about you Aunt Lee, when he left you for another woman and treated you so cruelly, by cutting you and your boys off financially? And how about when you told me he came home one day during this horrific period and threw you on the bed and raped you? You told me this when I was 17. You were like a second mother to me. I miss you.

Brian, what about the time your dad beat you so hard you had bruises on your face and your poor fearful mom put makeup on you so you could go off to your prep school? The beatings of all of you I witnessed. Ghost cousin Mark running with your muscular body away from your father as he chased you down like some wild animal. You were so much bigger than him. I understand for I couldn't hit back either, hiding the pain, year after year, I miss you also.

I had to go after your father with the law because of what he did to me, to you, to others. No guys, I'm not psychotic or "crazy," I have seen too many doctors to believe that one. Depression, post traumatic stress disorder, fibromyalgia, migraine sufferer, asthmatic, TMJ from clenching and opening my little mouth too wide, these are my wounds. I'll never understand why I didn't form a psychosis. Memory is strange, some events may be jumbled, the colors a different hue. Yet I speak the truth that I know. I was never prodded or poked by someone else's agenda to remember. It just came, as if I gave birth to three whales. Funny how after my son Jake's birth it all came flooding back, I couldn't stop the tsunami of memory. All of the help that I got from investigators corroborated my intuitions. There were other victims also. I found them. As the puzzle was put together, after years of not trusting myself, it all made sense…finally.

It happened my sweet family, it just happened.

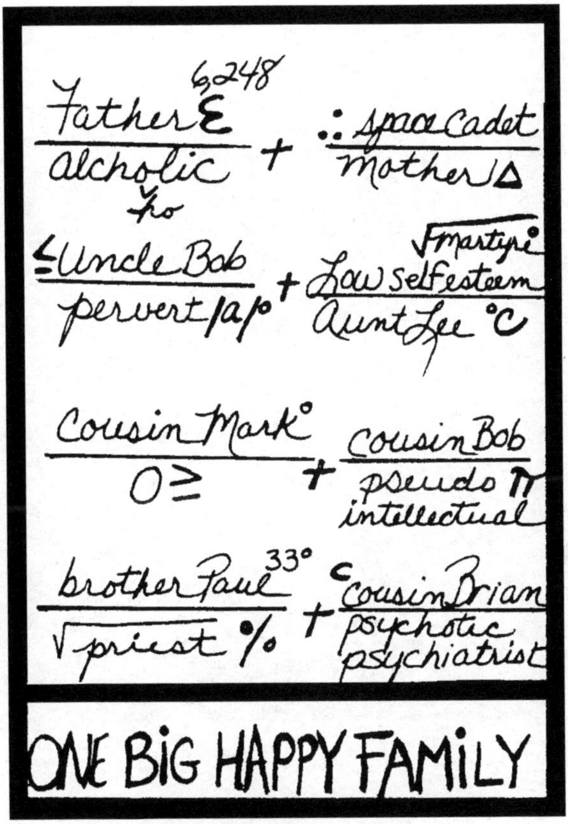

The Theory of Relativity

Sally has finally found
her roots... now she is content

If She Would Only Take Off Her Ring

When I look at my beautiful mother today, I see a woman with strength and serenity, a woman I would hope to become. As I am forced to close my eyes and remember, forced by my own need to be whole and well, without excruciating migraines, so that I can be the woman my mom has become, I must face painful memories of who she was. My mother was a very sick person until her mid-for-ties. She suffered from two terrible diseases, alcoholism and depression. A double, yet common combination that makes it's victims suffer so deeply they doubt the value of their own lives, I know, I've inherited these diseases.

My mother, like myself, would prefer to whitewash the past between us. So many other people to be angry with: daddy for not being there, Uncle Bob for his sexual abuse. Bob is an especially gruesome and easy catch-all for every negative "thing" of the past. So, as painful as it is, I must push to the most excruciating taboo territory, THE MOTHERLAND. I must vomit my way through this sacred ground.

Coming home from school in second, third, fourth and even fifth grade would always be a "What's behind door number two?" day upon entering my house. I never knew what I would find. That is to say, I never knew what mood, what condition my mother would be in. Some days would be fine, she would be "normal" and I could breathe a sigh of short comfort. Other days, I had to read the subtle signs of moods that could possibly shift the evening from a safe place to a place of hell, even a place where blood was spilled. There was the night mom was trying to open a can. With her shaking hands she cut herself so that blood gushed everywhere. I remember her slurred, drunken, whining voice telling me not to be so dramatic as I desperately tried to reach for the phone to call grandma or someone because this was an emergency! Mommy was bleeding to death (so I thought, what eight-year-old wouldn't?) I was so frantic as she slapped me away from the phone, both our squeals of fear floating up to a silent God. The memory ends with the sound of squealing pigs or that funny noise people make when imitating the shower scene in the movie Psycho.

And me, the mother to my children. There was a day when I was dealing with my demons. I had just found out the last details about my uncle. The strain and tear on my marriage, on my body, on my family became so heavy that in one impulsive, accumulated, horrific moment, I took a handful of Xanax as my two-year-old son bounced on my bed. But you see, I was luckier than my mother, I had a nanny for my children and she was able to scoop up my son after I told her what I had done, and she literally saved my life. Thank you, Amy Rose.

We mothers, who are filled with shame, can heal. We can free ourselves from the guilt and shame if we have the courage to face ourselves.

Mom, I so wanted to ask you as you were hitting me away from the phone, "Would you please take off your ring?" Your hands were too weak to hurt me. I had already found my safe quiet place in myself that I had with Bob. It was that damn ring. I couldn't catch my breath through the sobs to tell you. That damn ring. I wanted you to please take it off.

I forgive you mom, for you were trapped by your own demons just like I was. We are no different. Please accept this writing as a gift of honesty for you so that you too can let go of your guilt and forgive yourself, as I forgive myself, and so on through the ages of mothers who hurt both themselves and those they love most.

I forgive you, as I hope my children will forgive me, so we can all rest in the gift of compassion. I love you dear mother. You have owned up, you strong, beautiful being. I accept your apology, for I understand.

Bingo And Grandma

My grandma, who spoke broken English, came to America from Poland at the age of 16. She had eight children. Four-year-old Michael died in her arms. She was the most loving, spiritual, saintly person I have ever known. She was non judgmental, and yet a daily communicant, daily mediator, daily grandma. Beautiful roly-poly tiny grandma, who smelled like all good grandmas. I would wrap my arms around her tiny body and sniff myself into a state of bliss.

Grandma's one night of indulgence was Bingo. There she would be with her three cards and a sack full of pennies sitting silently, hopefully, happily, beautifully. I loved to go with my grandma to Bingo. To this day, I still play the game. My educated, sophisticated friends lovingly laugh at me for trudging off to play, rain or snow, at least once a week. Bingo is a gold mine of spectacular women who bond and talk about how they never win, what they cooked for dinner, about their life's joys and sorrows. Week to week we bond and get to know each other and care about each other's lives and daub away and laugh — oh how we laugh and root each other on and say "shit" when we need one number and they don't call it. These women are human beings, soulful books unto themselves.

People laugh at the notion of little gray haired Bingo Ladies and dismiss their lives with a thought. But oh my friends take time to look into just one lady's eyes and you will feel a lifetime. We come to join each other to forget our sadness and that smoky church hall becomes our safe, therapeutic haven.

Thank you grandma for loving me so, in the middle of the madness, for taking me to Bingo, for letting me take the Easter basket to be blessed. Thanks for your Polish soul food, gumkies and chaadninna, dumplings and pierogies. You knew I was suffering. Thank you for letting me wash your dentures as you lay dying of leukemia…brushing away the bright orange carrot pieces that you ate with no hunger, thinking that carrots might save your life. Oh, I understand, for I thought Roy Rogers would save mine. We surviving optimists with our frightened souls. Soul to soul...me and you...then and now.

They tell me you died with your arms extended to God with a smile on your face. No surprise to me, just comfort remembering this beautiful painting.

So if you ever dismiss gray haired old ladies who play Bingo, remember my Grandma, Louise Rogala-Maras.

Genius Bingo

Something To Think About

May I suggest something that helps me be grateful, heal, and rise above my pain? We survivors have been blessed with the earned ability to feel deep compassion. It was once told to me that religion is for people who want to avoid going to hell, and spirituality is for people who have already been there. Today, as I raise my children, I have time to do some volunteer work. I have chosen hospice work. I had thought about this over the years and finally took some action and trained to become a part of the hospice team. I also am involved in a spiritual caregiver's group that tends to the belief systems and spiritual needs of our patients. I have the privilege of bathing the patients, holding their hands at the moment they transition from life to death, stroking their heads, comforting their families. It helps me get outside myself and give from that rich resource of suffering that we share. "For it is in giving that we receive." So said St. Francis of Assisi. No, I am not trying to be a saint these days but a human being who sometimes can transcend her own humanness by sharing her pain and her compassion with others.

We survivors can be too hard on ourselves, feel like ugly animals with our low self-esteem, with our injured bodies and souls. Yet we can, for moments, transcend our humanness by giving of ourselves to others who suffer. Feeding the homeless, working with AIDS patients, caring for hospice patients, volunteering at a rape center, I promise you, soul sisters and brothers, it works.

"Ignatius of Loyola,
Theresa of Avila,
John of the Cross,
Francis of Assisi.
Every Saint has taught the paradox that lies
at the heart of the spiritual life:
To live passionately, but with freedom of spirit that
does not cling even to life Itself."

———

Sister Helen Prejean, from Dead Man Walking

To Mom and Dad

Have no remorse, for it took me a long time to tell you. Do not blame yourselves, you didn't know what was really going on. I have always respected and loved you so, for the people you are: good, loving parents. It didn't surprise me that when I finally told all, chapter and verse, you didn't blink an eye of disbelief. You believed me as we sobbed together. You are so brave to face the past with me.

I love you and I thank you.

Fear...Still

I actually had a fleeting fear that I might be killed for writing this book. I wasn't going to address this, but of course I knew I had too. It is a recurring theme with us survivors, a gnawing, never forgotten fear instilled by our perpetrators who invariably threatened that horrible things would happen to us if we told. We all have scars, and of course in writing this piece I scratched mine open a bit. Yet, I'm gonna tell, tell, tell...to those who want to listen. This is a lifelong task. We must learn to embrace our fears, ourselves, our memories, our pain. The more we gain the courage to be truthful and tell, even only to ourselves, the more we can begin to be free. Just the belief in our knowing is probably the most powerful of all antidotes to fear.

He always knew he
was different.

A Letter of Love and Respect to My Fellow Survivors

I love you, I love us. We are so strong to have lived this far – no matter how scared and scarred you are, no matter whether you are in a psych ward somewhere like I was, battling my dragon named Bob. Go on...cry if you can. Even if you think it will never end, even if snot flows from your nose and your stomach hurts, rainbows will begin to appear. And remember, sweet siblings, our souls are one, we are not alone. And laugh, it's o.k., come on. Ha Ha Ha, watch a funny movie, read Norman Cousin's Anatomy of an Illness. Come on, we can laugh, if not now...someday, I promise, you will laugh again. Out of our ashes we can build a new form, a new love for ourselves, because we are alive and our pain can subside. Laugh...oh...please learn to laugh at the absurdity of our situations. Open our soaked eyes to the beauty and joy that is before us. HA HA HA...come on, you can do it. A half a smile will do, a tear will do, wherever you are is perfect and it will do.

I love you and I admire your strength to face your devils and look them in the eyes. YOU are my heroes, YOU are my soul mates. We know each other and this book is a gift to honor you my sweet beautiful loves.

71

Put On Your Tap Shoes

Me…and…my…mi…graines…strolling through life
pain…ful…leeeeeeee.
I have done…
Midrin
Indocin
Aspirin
Confessed my sins
Biofeedback
Lying on back
Ice packs
Bees wax
Beta blockers
Doctors Doctors
Doctors Doctors
Doctors Doctors.
Blaming Bob
Hating God
Hating bod
Trod…trod…trod…
Thru the pain
Feel so lame

So much shame
Rack my brain
For the cause Land of Oz???
Take a pause.......
To break that vase
On my head
Wish me dead
Sick of bed
GODDAMN HEAD!!!
Hospitalize
Spiritualize
Realize
Acceptacize
Fioranol
Demoral
FUCK IT ALL!!!

————

Written between throwing up
from my millionth migraine.

Hatred

Hate Hate Hate Hate Hate Hate red red red red red red red. I know a heart filled with hatred. I know a head filled with severe chronic pain. Pain that got me hooked on pills, pain that keeps the pain from leaving because hate and good and Catholic don't go together. The word hate scares me to write down because if I have true hate in my heart, what is next? If I give up the internalized form of good Catholic hate called migraines where does it go? One cannot act out on hate. I hatehatehateheatehethat gahkn;ljz;l/kzj hpioae5poajpmn5e!!! HATE.

I hate you, Dr. Bob. You can have my physical pain for I just can not take it any more. I am tired of doctors and pain clinics and medicine and psychiatrists to help me figure out where the physical pain comes from. If I do one more exercise on pain I promise you I will have to become a yogi or that guy who seems to be on TV a lot lately sticking pins and sharp objects through his cheeks and other various parts of his body. I am not a guru or a yogi or a saint, I am not a pin cushion or a table or a can of paint. I am a hater who hates and has headaches from the hate, so go away hate so no more headaches, or keep the headaches and keep the hate.

NOOOOOOOOOOOOOOOOOOOOOOOOOOOOOOOOOO!! !!!

I did call the licensing bureau and was able to file a complaint against my uncle only because I was once his patient. I was informed by a lawyer working on the case, that they had a huge file on my uncle and that it had become a "TOP PRIORITY" case. It was being prepared for the state attorney general. They had their investigators on the case. I began my own investigation (a dangerous thing to do). I reported my findings on a daily basis to this lawyer.

Bob, Dear Uncle Bob, Wise Doctor Bob. I heard you were exchanging drugs for sex with teenagers. I heard it from someone who was one of your clients who was afraid for his life to talk to me. Why is it that everyone around your criminal activities is afraid to talk to me? My scared, junkie friend said he would tell me what happened only after I begged him and swore that it was safe because all I was trying to do was find other rape victims of my uncle's so I could get a case against him. He told me the story. He told me he was in Bob's office (and of course we know all those many years he never ever had a receptionist or a nurse). He told me he was sitting around waiting for his scrip, as the office was kind of like a hangout for junkies. He told me many men with BIG letters that said DEA on their jackets dragged Bob out like a fool, one man on each side. He told me how everyone was so frightened and no one spoke a word out of fear. They were all shocked that nothing was in the paper the next day or any other day ever never ever after that. This person was clean and sober when he told me. He was afraid for his family and his life to tell me more. This person, my "deep throat," gave me a huge gift of information. Thank you "this person."

I told this story to a friend of my mother's who worked with young addicts in my uncle's hometown. In telling me his story he broke confidentiality rules of therapy because he thought he could help. It seems that Bob's name came up over and over in therapy because of his sexual abuses, but that this was all confidential. So my uncle's name was kept behind confidential doors because his other victims had their own guilt with their drug addictions; or perhaps they had lovers and mothers who knew nothing of this soooooooo let's keep quiet, let's whisper so Lori can get headaches that take her to the emergency room over and over and over because the pain is too great.

This friend gave me the number of someone in the FBI so that they could "help" me. This was on a Sunday. Early Monday morning I got a call. The gentleman introduced himself and asked me what I knew. I trustingly told him everything. He asked for each phone number of every person that I had spoken with. After he had gathered his information, he said "stay out of this drug stuff, it's very dangerous." "You may have a civil case, for your own safety pursue the civil case." I tried to call the lawyer from the licensing bureau that same day. After speaking to her on a daily basis over several months she would not take my call or answer my letters. No one would talk to me.

I guess I should have known that my life would be in danger if I told, just like Bob threatened way back then. I shouldn't have been surprised when I woke up and in front of my house was painted the outline of a dead body, or when my brakes failed one day. In retrospect they saved my life and their case. I needed to tell you this my dear friends because I have always been afraid that he would come and kill me if I did. That's why I'M GONNA TELL.

About a year later a huge story broke in the local paper. A story about a doctor, not my uncle, who was convicted for some of the crimes my uncle committed only somehow he was a person more important to the FBI. I guess that my uncle was a small fish in the pond and snitched.

Seven years later, before I decided to put this book into print, I needed help to close this chapter in my life. I hired a top private investigator to help me close the door. HE FOUND NOTHING! Nothing! He said it seemed like everything had been wiped clean. The licensing bureau doesn't even have my complaint let alone the stack of information I was told they had years ago before the FBI was involved. When I began this book, I thought I had had Bob's license taken away, so the state investigators told me, and today in the year 2000, he still has his license. Boy was I played with and lied to and I hate hate hate these goddamn headaches!!!!!!

I did do the civil thing and went with my wonderful lawyers to try and "Get" him. This was long before newer laws for victims were in effect. Yet I believe, knowing my lawyers dedication to this case, that we, in some ways, began the beginning and helped pave the path for the abused. Many hours were spent by these lawyers and a penny was never charged. The letter that follows is a result of their hard work for our cause. At the time, I felt I had lost and was devastated, but today I see we had won. I share this letter with you my fellow survivors. I give this to you with love. We did the best we could my friends, we did the best we could.

LAW OFFICES

June 22, 1990

 M.D.

Dear Dr. [redacted]

This office has been retained by Lori Cardille-Rogal to review and investigate legal remedies she may have against you for damages she sustained as a child as a result of your sexual abuse of her.

As you are aware, Lori Cardille-Rogal is suffering from severe post-traumatic syndrome as a direct result of certain abuse she sustained while in your care during her childhood. Our initial investigation supports the conclusion that Lori Cardille-Rogal was a victim of child abuse and that she has been greatly damaged.

We have advised Lori that as a victim of child sexual abuse, certain remedies exist for her through the filing of a civil action against the person responsible for the damages she has sustained. After extensive meetings with Lori, we are continuing our investigation and are considering filing suit against you on her behalf. As I am sure you have been advised by your legal counsel, the filing of these actions is governed by a two year statute of limitations. We have advised Lori that generally the two year statute of limitations begins when injury actually occurs. However, we have also advised Lori that Pennsylvania, in general tort actions, has also adopted the discovery rule which means that the cause of action does not begin until one knew or should have known about the injury that was sustained. Because Lori, like many adult-survivors of child sexual abuse, did not really have clear memories, and was not able to identify your conduct as child sexual abuse until much later in her life, we are now investigating exactly when the statute of limitations began in Lori's case and whether or not she still can maintain an action against you. We have advised Lori that although she may not ultimately be successful, as our office has been involved in many aspects of litigation regarding sexual abuse, and as there is currently no case law in Pennsylvania with regard to the discovery rule in these actions, we are most interested in possibly pursuing her case as a test case in this area.

We are sending this letter to you as part of this investigation, as a courtesy, in order that you are not surprised in the event you are made aware of any investigative work being done about you in the area where you live and where you formally practiced. It is our suggestion that if you believe you have appropriate insurance that covers your past conduct, you now notify your carrier so that you conform with applicable notice requirements of any policies. Likewise, we suggest that you make your legal counsel aware of our ongoing investigation and potential suit in order that you can

███████ M.D.
June 22, 1990
Page 2

be fully apprised of your rights in the event you are contacted by anyone on our behalf.

As you apparently know, Lori's process of attempting to heal from the wounds she has suffered, has been a long one and has been one that literally has cost her thousands of dollars. It is becoming clear that filing an action against you may be a very vital part of this healing process. We intend to do everything possible to continue our investigation for Lori and help her make some determination as to whether or not suit is feasible. Obviously, whether or not a legal determination is ultimately made, will not diminish your responsibility for your acts.

Very truly yours,

███████████████

███████

ALB:bp

cc: Ms. Lori Cardille-Rogal and James Rogal

October 4, 1990

Bob,

I feel compelled to write and let you know that "I know"
of the verbal, physical and sexual abuse you victimized
Lori with when she was a child. I know you did the things
Lori says you did. As a medical man, you are aware that
denial is a classic defense for someone who perpetrates
these actions on defenseless little girls. You started
your defense years ago by cleverly impugning (or at least
making a big effort to do so) Lori's veracity by talking
about her. A good offense is the best defense, and you
have used this for years in attempting to tear down her
credibility. In spite of this you did not succeed in
destroying Lori. She is a successful, loving human being.
Her success in both her career and her personal life is
admirable especially considering her tortuous memories
of your immoral actions.

However, the suffering does continue.

Do you know the suffering your actions have caused to Lori
as a child and an adult? I should have been there for her.
I thought I was protecting her, but I never suspected a
trusted "Uncle" would betray a child by perversion.

How you can walk around, act as though nothing happened,
reiterate that everything Lori says is a figment of her
imagination and pretend you are innocent of her accusations,
is beyond my comprehension.

Bob, you cannot begin to imagine how much anger and hurt
I feel in this situation. Your picking on a defenseless
litle girl to satisfy your needs is something I will never
understand. I feel this is so much worse since you do have
the knowledge of what these acts cause in suffering.
This is something Lori and my family will have to live
with for the rest of our lives.
As you know, the mind and subconscious keep this an open
and festering wound - even though one would pray to forget.
I personally cannot forgive you and, needless to say,
never want to lay eyes on you again. I feel you did so
much worse than abuse my trust - the abuse of Lori is the
issue that is unforgivable.
We all know there is a higher power for judgement, and I
have no recourse other than to feel you will be judged on
the hurt and suffering you have caused.

Bill Cardiule

The Memory Recipe

My son Jake was born at St. Vincent's Hospital in New York City's Greenwich Village on September 29, 1987. Up until then I had had memories of my abuse, but not the full most horrifying parts. Repression can be a wonderful thing. My beautiful, complicated mind was protecting me so I could go on living. This primitive, yet welcomed defense saved me. Thank you mind.

Let the circuits begin to connect. Jake was born by Caesarean section due to the herpes virus. Good Catholic girls don't get VDs, now called STDs.

Time to bake.

Recipe

1) Begin with major unconscious shame
2) Add husband who was very abusive at this time
3) Mix in that I was in a quarantined room and found my meal trays in the hall in front of my door. (AIDS was still highly misunderstood and the kitchen staff figured that anyone quarantined was going to kill them just by breathing on them).
4) Slowly pour in feelings of being ostracized and diseased (a favorite for abuse victims).
5) Sprinkle in that I started coughing up blood and thought I was dying (The death theme, he told me he would kill me if I told).

Stir this all together in a blender and bake for two weeks post op and VOILA!!!!

THE POSTPARTUM MEMORY CAKE

Major Postpartum Depression

Back to another hospital to remember. My body remembered first. I had this horrible taste of metal or sperm in my mouth. I was still coughing up blood and a broncho-scope showed that I had severe bronchitis. The taste of sperm was so strong and so strange. To add to the morbid mixture, I kept feeling that something was constantly dripping down my chin. I truly believed I had lost my mind, until the memories were unleashed like a racehorse at the gate. They had been baked and were ready to be eaten. The finished beautiful, juicy, rich memory cake was begging to be sliced open.

There I was, 10 year old me, sitting on a toilet in his house, and he comes in, I remember he had a plaid shirt on...plaid shirt, plaid shirt...he walks towards me and pushes me to the ground, he yanks my long ponytail and my neck snaps backwards this huge thing coming toward my face – screen goes blank – moments later, I clutch the sink spitting, vomiting, crying. After this, I went out to play with my cousins, the forgetting begins immediately.

My beautiful Jake, his miraculous birth, helped me remember. Once the memories began to fill in, there was no turning back.

Through the years, flashbacks and full memories would form. At first I doubted my sanity until I began to explore how the mind works and held on to the wings of many professionals who helped me understand. I gave them a piece of the cake and they seemed very satisfied knowing they helped present and serve it. I must say, it tasted bittersweet.

Not So Black & White

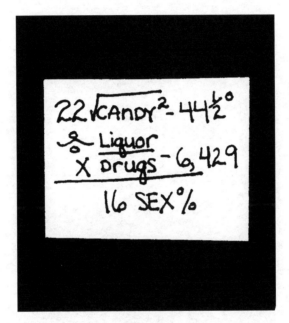

The seduction theory.

A guitar wishing
he was something
else.

What it's all about.

Epilogue

TRULY, SIMPLY, PROFOUNDLY... MR. ROGERS

As this book was about to go into print, I have once again been smashed flat to the ground not only as a pancake, but as a crepe. However, this is for the next book. I survived and am surviving still so no need to worry sweet friends.

THE Mr. Wonderful Rogers is a family friend. He is my husband's spiritual guru and my hero. After this past "me becoming a crepe" experience, I bumped into Fred and collapsed in his arms. So much the confused crying crepe that I was, I blurted out: "I'm so very sick, how do I stop from being a compulsive giver, I don't know how to heal myself this time." His response was like a mantra as he said to me "you're enough." These two words resonated at the core of my being. I continued to be held by him as I cried, as I began to settle down, his last words to me were: "just remember, you're enough," and he floated out the door. Thank you Mr. Rogers.

Mr. Rogers II

A few years ago, I was in Atlantic City at a Black Jack table and I made a good, yet wild, bet...lets just say I was taking a chance. This drunk fellow next to me yelled "Where do you think you live? Mr. Rogers' neighborhood?" I slowly turned my head to him and said: "to tell you the truth, I do." Of course he thought I was being a smart ass. The truth is the truth is the truth...my truth, your own truth. Lets keep listening with our internal stethoscopes to that silent deep knowing. We know.

The Endendum

A special note of love to my mother. To share what I did about my memory of her is not an easy thing for her, yet she said if I had to do it for me to heal, then do it. Her courage through her own illness as well as my loving father, flatly, plainly, "blows me away." My mother may be the strongest person I know. She saved my life many a time through my toughest times. My father was always loving and kind.

I love you Louise and Chilly Billy.
I love you Mom and Dad.

About The Author

Lori currently lives in Pittsburgh, Pennsylvania with her husband Jim Rogal and her children Kate and Jake.

It is not one person who has it all together...
It is all together that we become one person.
We need each other.

The Author

The End...

The Beginning...

Made in the USA
Middletown, DE
25 May 2016